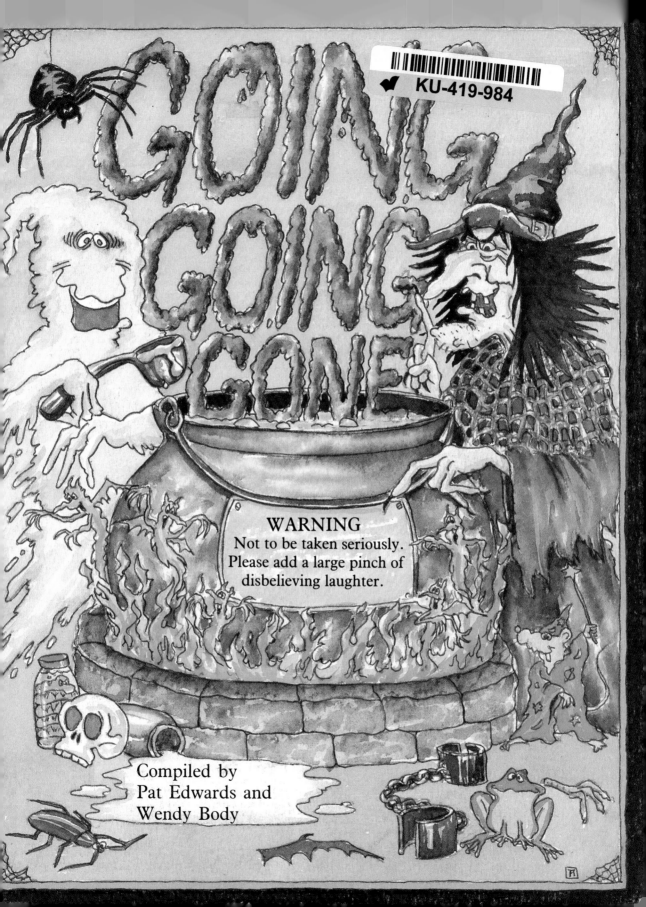

KU-419-984

GOING GOING GOING GONE

WARNING
Not to be taken seriously.
Please add a large pinch of
disbelieving laughter.

Compiled by
Pat Edwards and
Wendy Body

Acknowledgements
We are grateful to the following for permission to reproduce copyright material: The author's agents for the story 'Jimmy Takes Vanishing Lessons' by Walter R Brooks from *Haunted Houseful* by Alfred Hitchcock; Dolphin Concert Productions Ltd for the poem 'Oh I Wish I'd Looked After Me Teeth' from *Some of Me Poems* by Pam Ayres, Copyright Pam Ayres; William Heinemann and the author's agents for the story 'Uninvited Ghosts' from *Uninvited Ghosts and Other Stories* by Penelope Lively © Penelope Lively 1981, (first published in *Frank and Polly Muir's Big Dipper*, Heinemann 1981); the author's agents for the story 'Just Imagine' by Eunice McMullen, Copyright Eunice & Nigel McMullen 1981; Scholastic-TAB Publications Ltd for extract from pp. 79-89 *The Toothpaste Genie* by Frances Duncan, Copyright 1981 by Frances Duncan, (pub Scholastic-TAB Publications Ltd);

the author's agents for the story 'Lazy Tok' from *The Meeting Pool* by Mervyn Skipper. Pages 74-5 were written by Wendy Body.

We are grateful to the following for permission to reproduce photographs: BBC Hulton Picture Library, page 74 *above right*; John Chalcraft, page 74 *below left*; City of Bristol, pages 74 *below right*, 75 *below left* and *below right*; Compix, Commonwealth Institute, page 37; Douglas Dickens, page 35 *below*; Colin Molyneux, page 74 *above left*; RV Pandit for The Perennial Press, *Ganga — Sacred River of India* (photo Raghubir Singh) page 35 *above*; David Scharf Photography, page 56; Reece Winstone, page 75 *above*.

Illustrators, other than those acknowledged with each story, include Thomas Atkinson pp.4-9; Jean Cooper-Brown pp.24-5 and pp.92-3; Cheryl Tarbuck pp.32-7; David Bone pp.58-9 and pp.88-91; Chris Ryley pp.60-6; Frances Lloyd pp.74-5; Ian Forss pp.94-6.

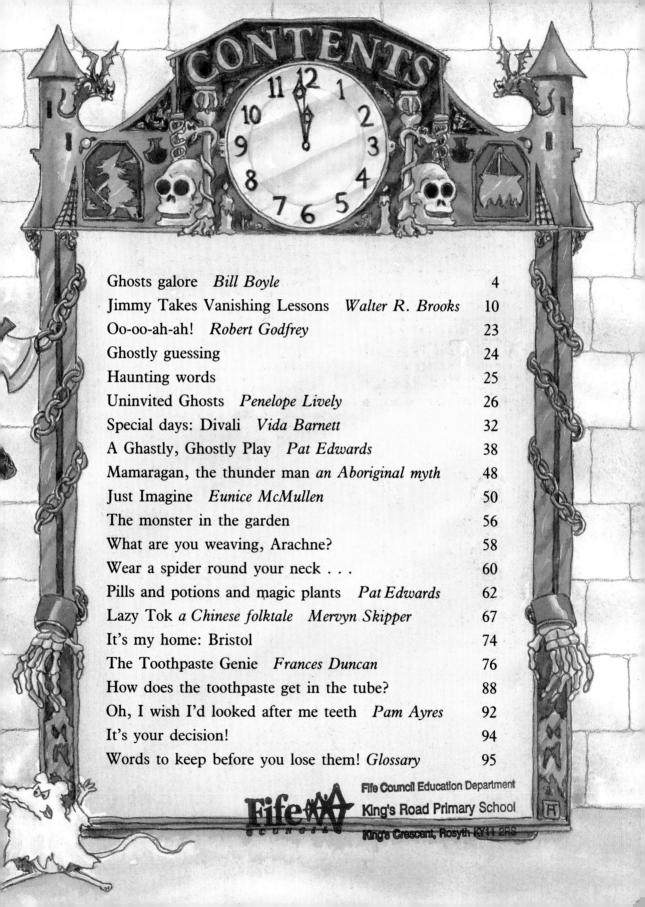

CONTENTS

Fife Council Education Department
King's Road Primary School
King's Crescent, Rosyth KY11 2RS

GHOSTS GALORE

A Royal Ghost

> I am Anne Boleyn's ghost. I was married to King Henry VIII. He had me beheaded in 1536 but I have returned to visit my old haunts regularly.

People have often thought that they have seen the ghost of Anne Boleyn in the Tower of London. On one occasion, in 1933, a sentry heard her footsteps. When he saw her headless body, he tried to stop her. His bayonet passed right through her!

On the anniversary of her execution (May 19th), it is said that Anne arrives at Blickling Hall, near Norwich, in a coach driven by four headless coachmen. She is holding her head in her lap!

Each Christmas Eve, Anne's ghost is supposed to cross the bridge at Hever Castle in Kent where she spent her childhood.

Ghost Animals

In East Anglia, the ghost of Black Shuck, the Demon Dog, roams at sunset. With his bright red eyes gleaming in the dusk, he is a terrifying sight to the people who believe that they have seen him.

In the winter of 1816, a sentry on night duty inside the Jewel House of the Tower of London saw the shape of a huge bear entering the room. He struck his bayonet into the animal's body, but it went straight through and stuck in the door!

The stuffed head of a bull terrier guards the bar of the Star Inn at Ingatestone, Essex. The ghost of the terrier is said to haunt the passage leading to the bar. Many people have reported that when they take their dogs into the bar, their hair bristles as though they are afraid.

On Christmas Eve, a bus from Barnstaple to Lynton in Devon could not stop when a black dog and two sheep suddenly appeared in front of it. The driver got out to look, expecting to find the animals dead on the road, but there was nothing there.

Sandford Orcas

The ancient manor house at Sandford Orcas in Dorset has everything that you would expect to find in a haunted house.

According to certain people, the house is filled with ghosts. There are fourteen ghosts altogether, including a lady in green, a monk, an Elizabethan lady, a ghost footman, not to mention a ghost dog!

Banquo's Ghost

William Shakespeare wrote plays in the sixteenth and early seventeenth centuries. He is one of the most famous writers who ever lived. One of his plays is called *Macbeth*.

In the play, Macbeth is a general who serves the Scottish king, Duncan. One day, Macbeth, with his friend Banquo, meets three witches who tell him that he will become the King of Scotland. Macbeth is ambitious and he decides to make sure this will happen by killing King Duncan himself. At night he goes into the King's bedroom and kills him.

Macbeth becomes the King. But he is a frightened man. He is scared that others will find out about his dreadful deed, particularly his friend Banquo. Macbeth arranges for two men to kill Banquo and his son. On the night Banquo is killed, Macbeth holds a big feast for the noblemen and lords of the castle. As they are all sitting round the table Macbeth sees Banquo's ghost. Nobody else sees it. What do you think this means?

Jimmy takes vanishing lessons

THE school bus picked up Jimmy Crandall every morning at the side road that led up to his aunt's house, and every afternoon it dropped him there again. And so twice a day, on the bus, he passed the entrance to the mysterious road.

It wasn't much of a road any more. It was choked with weeds and blackberry bushes, and the woods on both sides pressed in so closely that the branches met overhead, and it was dark and gloomy even on bright days. The bus driver once pointed it out.

"Folks that go in there after dark," he said, "well, they usually don't ever come out again. There's a haunted house about a quarter of a mile down that road." He paused. "But you ought to know about that, Jimmy. It was your grandfather's house."

Jimmy knew about it, and he knew that it now belonged to his Aunt Mary. But Jimmy's aunt would never talk to him about the house. She said the stories about it were silly nonsense and there were no such things as ghosts. If all the villagers weren't a lot of superstitious idiots, she would be able to let the house, and then she would have enough money to buy Jimmy some decent clothes and take him to the cinema.

Jimmy thought it was all very well to say that there were no such things as ghosts, but how about the people who had tried to live there? Aunt Mary had let the house three times, but every family had moved out within a week. They said the things that went on there were just too queer. So nobody would live in it any more.

Jimmy thought about the house a lot. If he could only prove that there wasn't a ghost . . . And one Saturday when his aunt was in the village, Jimmy took the key to the haunted house from its hook on the kitchen door, and started out.

It had seemed like a fine idea when he had first thought of it — to find out for himself. Even in the silence and damp gloom of the old road it still seemed pretty good. Nothing to be scared of, he told himself. Ghosts aren't around in the daytime. But when he came out in the clearing and looked at those blank, dusty windows, he wasn't so sure.

"Oh come on!" he told himself. And he squared his shoulders and waded through the long grass to the porch.

Then he stopped again. His feet did not seem to want to go up the steps. It took him nearly five minutes to persuade them to move. But when at last they did, they marched right up and across the porch to the front door, and Jimmy set his teeth hard and put the key in the keyhole. It turned with a squeak. He pushed the door open and went in.

That was probably the bravest thing that Jimmy had ever done. He was in a long dark hall with closed doors on both sides, and on the right there were stairs going up. He had left the door open behind him, and the light from it showed him that, except for the hat-rack and table and chairs, the hall was empty. And then as he stood there, listening to the bumping of his heart, gradually the light faded, the hall grew darker and darker — as if something huge had come up on the porch behind him and stood there, blocking the door way. He swung round quickly, but there was nothing there.

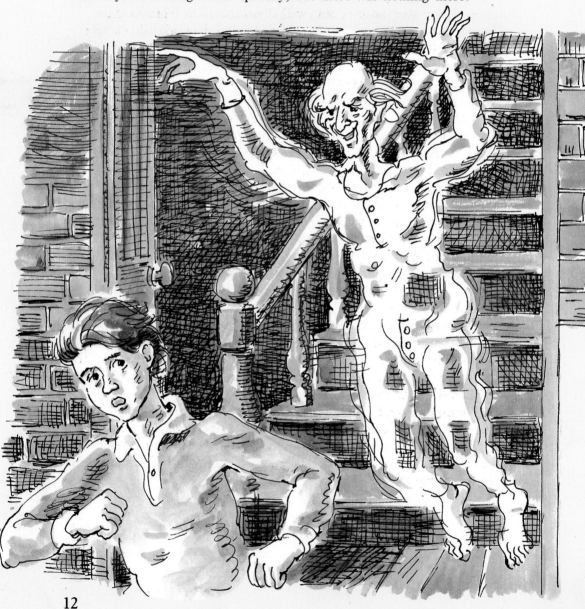

He drew a deep breath. It must have been just a cloud passing across the sun. But then the door, all by itself, began to swing shut. And before he could stop it, it closed with a bang. And it was then, as he was pulling frantically at the handle to get out, that Jimmy saw the ghost.

It behaved just as you would expect a ghost to behave. It was a tall, dim, white figure, and it came gliding slowly down the stairs towards him. Jimmy gave a yell, yanked the door open, and tore down the steps.

He didn't stop until he was well down the road. Then he had to get his breath. He sat down on a log. "Boy!" he said. "I've seen a ghost! Golly, was that awful!" Then after a minute he thought, "What was so awful about it? He was trying to scare me, like that smart aleck who was always jumping out from behind things. Pretty silly business for a grown-up ghost to be doing."

It always makes you cross when someone deliberately tries to scare you. And as Jimmy got over his fright, he began to get angry. And pretty soon he got up and started back. "I must get that key, anyway," he thought, for he had left it in the door.

This time he approached very quietly. He thought he'd just lock the door and go home. But as he tiptoed up the steps he saw it was still open; and as he reached out cautiously for the key, he heard a faint sound. He drew back and peeped round the door-jamb, and there was the ghost.

The ghost was going back upstairs, but he wasn't gliding now, he was doing a sort of dance, and every other step he would bend double and shake with laughter. His thin cackle was the sound Jimmy had heard. Evidently he was enjoying the joke he had played.

That made Jimmy crosser than ever. He stuck his head farther around the door-jamb and yelled "Boo!" at the top of his lungs. The ghost gave a thin shriek and leaped two feet in the air, then collapsed on the stairs.

As soon as Jimmy saw he could scare the ghost even worse than the ghost could scare him, he wasn't afraid any more and he came right into the hall. The ghost was hanging on the banister and panting. "Oh, my goodness!" he gasped. "Oh my gracious! Boy, you can't do that to me!"

"I did it, didn't I?" said Jimmy. "Now we're even."

"Nothing of the kind," said the ghost crossly. "You seem pretty stupid, even for a boy. Ghosts are supposed to scare people. People aren't supposed to scare ghosts." He got up slowly and glided down and sat on the bottom step. "But look here, boy; this could be pretty serious for me if people got to know about it."

"You mean you don't want me to tell anybody about it?" Jimmy asked.

"Suppose we make a deal," the ghost said. "You keep quiet about this, and in return I'll — well, let's see; how would you like to know how to vanish?"

"Oh, that would be swell!" Jimmy exclaimed. "But — can you vanish?"

"Sure", said the ghost, and he did. All at once he just wasn't there. Jimmy was alone in the hall.

But his voice went right on. "It would be pretty handy, wouldn't it?" he said persuasively. "You could get into the cinema free whenever you wanted to, and if your aunt called you to do something — when you were in the garden, say — well, she wouldn't be able to find you."

"I don't mind helping Aunt Mary," Jimmy said.

"H'm. High-minded, eh?" said the ghost. "Well, then . . ."

"I wish you'd please reappear," Jimmy interrupted. "It makes me feel funny to talk to somebody who isn't there."

"Sorry, I forgot," said the ghost, and there he was again, sitting on the bottom step. Jimmy could see the step, dimly, right through him. "Good trick, eh? Well, if you don't like vanishing, maybe I could teach you to seep through keyholes. Like this." He floated over to the door and went right through the keyhole, the way water goes down the drain. Then he came back the same way.

"That's useful, too," he said. "Getting into locked rooms and so on. You can go anywhere the wind can."

"No," said Jimmy. "There's only one thing you can do to get me to promise not to tell about scaring you. Go and live somewhere else. There's Miller's up the road. Nobody lives there any more."

"That old shack!" said the ghost, with a nasty laugh. "Doors and windows half off, roof leaky — no thanks! What do you think it's like in a storm, windows banging, rain dripping on you — I guess not! Peace and quiet, that's really what a ghost wants out of life."

"Well, I don't think it's very fair," Jimmy said, "for you to live in a house that doesn't belong to you and keep my aunt from letting it."

"Pooh!" said the ghost. "I'm not stopping her from letting it. I don't take up any room, and it's not my fault if people get scared and leave."

"It certainly is!" Jimmy said angrily. "You don't play fair and I'm not going to make any bargain with you. I'm going to tell everybody how I scared you."

"Oh, you mustn't do that!" The ghost seemed quite disturbed and he vanished and reappeared rapidly several times. "If that got out, every ghost in the country would be in terrible trouble."

So they argued about it. The ghost said if Jimmy wanted money he could learn to vanish; then he could join a circus and get a big salary. Jimmy said he didn't want to be in a circus; he wanted to go to college and learn to be a doctor. He was very firm. And the ghost began to cry. "But this is my home, boy," he said. "Thirty years I've lived here and no trouble to anybody, and now you want to throw me out into the cold world! And for what? A little money! That's pretty heartless." And he sobbed, trying to make Jimmy feel cruel.

Jimmy didn't feel cruel at all, for the ghost had certainly driven plenty of other people out into the cold world. But he didn't really think it would do much good for him to tell anybody that he had scared the ghost. Nobody would believe him, and how could he prove it? So after a minute he said, "Well, all right. You teach me to vanish and I won't tell." They settled it that way.

Jimmy didn't say anything to his aunt about what he'd done. But every Saturday he went to the haunted house for his vanishing lesson. It is really quite easy when you know how, and in a couple of weeks he could flicker, and in six weeks the ghost gave him an examination and he got a B plus, which is very good for a human. So he thanked the ghost and shook hands with him and said, "Well, goodbye now. You'll hear from me."

"What do you mean by that?" said the ghost suspiciously. But Jimmy just laughed and ran off home.

That night at supper Jimmy's aunt said, "Well what have you been doing today?"

"I've been learning to vanish."

His aunt smiled and said, "That must be fun."

"Honestly," said Jimmy. "The ghost up a Grandfather's house taught me."

"I don't think that's very funny," said his aunt. "And will you please not — why, where are you? " she demanded, for he had vanished.

"Here, Aunt Mary," he said as he reappeared.

"Merciful heavens!" she exclaimed, and she pushed back her chair and rubbed her eyes hard. Then she looked at him again.

Well, it took a lot of explaining and he had to do it twice more before he could persuade her that he really could vanish. She was pretty upset. But at last she calmed down and they had a long talk. Jimmy kept his word and didn't tell her that he had scared the ghost, but he said he had a plan and at last, though very reluctantly, she agreed to help him.

So the next day she went up to the old house and started to work. She opened the windows and swept and dusted and aired the bedding and made as much noise as possible. This disturbed the ghost, and pretty soon he came floating into the room where she was sweeping. She was scared all right. She gave a yell and threw the broom at him. As the broom went right through him and he came nearer, waving his arms and groaning, she shrank back.

And Jimmy, who had been standing there invisible all the time, suddenly appeared and jumped at the ghost with a 'Boo!' and the ghost fell over in a dead faint.

As soon as Jimmy's aunt saw that, she wasn't frightened any more. She found some smelling salts and held them under the ghost's nose, and when he came to she tried to help him into a chair. Of course, she couldn't help him. But at last he sat up and said reproachfully to Jimmy, "You broke your word!"

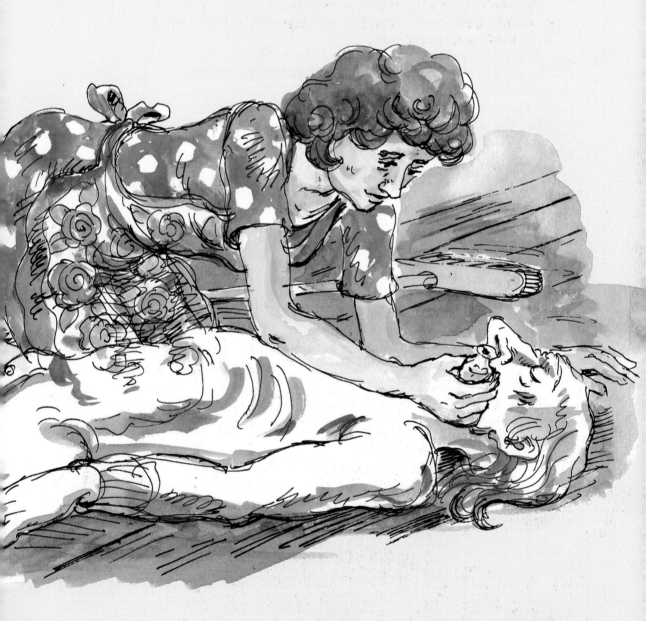

"I promised not to tell about scaring you!" said the boy, "but I didn't promise not to scare you again."

And his aunt said, "You really are a ghost, aren't you? I thought you were just stories people made up. Well, excuse me, but I must get on with my work." And she began sweeping and banging around with her broom harder than ever.

The ghost put his hands to his head. "All this noise," he said. "Couldn't you work more quietly, ma'am?"

"Whose house is this, anyway?" she demanded. "If you don't like it, why don't you move out?"

The ghost sneezed violently several times. "Excuse me," he said. "You're raising so much dust. Where's that boy?" he asked suddenly. For Jimmy had vanished again.

"I'm sure I don't know," she replied. "Probably getting ready to scare you again."

"You ought to have better control of him," said the ghost severely. "If he was my boy, I'd take a hairbrush to him."

"You have my permission," she said, and she reached right through the ghost and pulled the chair cushion out from under him and began banging the dust out of it. "What's more," she went on, as he got up and glided wearily to another chair, "Jimmy and I are going to sleep here at night from now on, and I don't think it would be very clever of you to try any tricks."

"Ha, ha," said the ghost nastily. "He who laughs last . . ."

"Ha, ha, yourself," said Jimmy's voice from close behind him. "And that's me, laughing last."

The ghost muttered and vanished.

Jimmy's aunt put cottonwool in her ears and slept that night in the best bedroom with the light lit. The ghost screamed for a while down in the cellar, but nothing happened, so he came upstairs. He thought he would appear to her as two glaring, fiery eyes, which was one of his best tricks, but first he wanted to be sure where Jimmy was. But he couldn't find him. He hunted all over the house and, though he was invisible himself, he got more and more nervous. He kept imagining that at any moment Jimmy might jump out at him from some dark corner and scare him into fits. Finally he got so jittery that he went back to the cellar and hid in the coal bin all night.

The following days were just as bad for the ghost. Several times he tried to scare Jimmy's aunt while she was working, but she didn't take any notice, and twice Jimmy managed to sneak up on him and appear suddenly with a loud yell, frightening him dreadfully. He was, I suppose, rather timid even for a ghost. He began to look quite haggard. He had several long arguments with Jimmy's aunt, in which he wept and appealed to her sympathy, but she was firm. If he wanted to live there he would have to pay rent, just like anybody else. There was the abandoned Miller farm two miles up the road. Why didn't he move there?

When the house was all in apple-pie order, Jimmy's aunt went down to the village to see a Mr and Mrs Whistler, who were living at the hotel because they couldn't find a house to move into. She told them about the old house, but they said, "No, thank you. We've heard about that house. It's haunted. I'll bet," they said, "you wouldn't dare spend a night there."

She told them that she had spent the last week there, but they evidently didn't believe her. So she said, "You know my nephew, Jimmy. He's twelve years old. I am so sure that the house is not haunted that, if you want to rent it, I will let Jimmy stay there with you every night until you are sure everything is all right."

"Ha!" said Mr Whistler. "The boy won't do it. He's got more sense."

So they sent for Jimmy. "Why, I've spent the last week there," he said. "Of course I will."

But the Whistlers still refused.

So Jimmy's aunt went round and told a lot of the village people about their talk, and everybody made so much fun of the Whistlers for being afraid, when a twelve-year-old boy wasn't, that they were ashamed, and said they would rent it. So they moved in.

Jimmy stayed there for a week, but he saw nothing of the ghost. And then one day one of the boys in his class told him that somebody had seen a ghost up at the Miller farm. So Jimmy knew the ghost had taken his aunt's advice.

Walter R. Brooks

Illustrated by David Pearson

Oo-oo-ah-ah!

A woman in a churchyard sat,
    Oo-oo-ah-ah!
Very short and very fat,
    Oo-oo-ah-ah!
She saw three corpses carried in,
    Oo-oo-ah-ah!
Very tall and very thin,
    Oo-oo-ah-ah!

Woman to the corpses said,
    Oo-oo-ah-ah!
Shall I be like you when I am dead?
    Oo-oo-ah-ah!
Corpses to the woman said,
    Oo-oo-ah-ah!
Yes, you'll be like us when you are dead,
    Oo-oo-ah-ah!
Woman to the corpses said —

                (Silence)

            Robert Godfrey

23

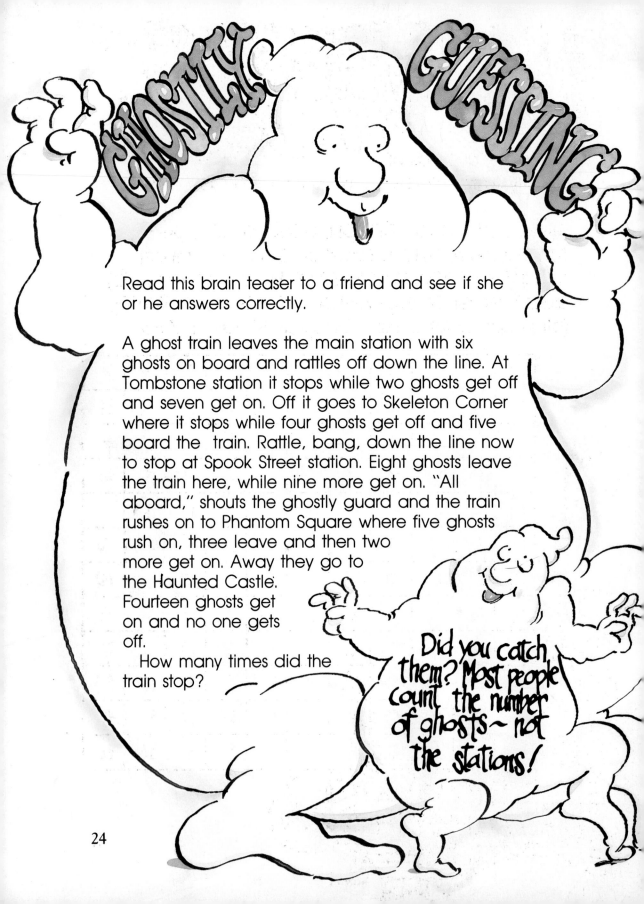

GHOSTLY GUESSING

Read this brain teaser to a friend and see if she or he answers correctly.

A ghost train leaves the main station with six ghosts on board and rattles off down the line. At Tombstone station it stops while two ghosts get off and seven get on. Off it goes to Skeleton Corner where it stops while four ghosts get off and five board the train. Rattle, bang, down the line now to stop at Spook Street station. Eight ghosts leave the train here, while nine more get on. "All aboard," shouts the ghostly guard and the train rushes on to Phantom Square where five ghosts rush on, three leave and then two more get on. Away they go to the Haunted Castle. Fourteen ghosts get on and no one gets off.

How many times did the train stop?

Did you catch them? Most people count the number of ghosts ~ not the stations!

HAUNTING WORDS

There are all kinds of ghostly words hidden in this puzzle. Can you find:

GRAVEYARD, MIST, DEMON, GENIE, SPIRIT, BOGY
(an evil spirit), GHOUL (another kind of nasty spirit),
VAMPIRE, SPOOK, WITCH, BANSHEE (a spirit that wails),
SKELETON, GHOSTS, PHANTOM, SPECTRE and WRAITH
(other names for ghosts), DREAMS, MOON, BONES.

G	E	N	I	E	A	T	Z	F	N	P
H	R	B	M	O	O	N	E	J	Q	H
O	B	A	R	D	B	S	V	X	U	A
U	O	N	V	R	O	B	A	W	F	N
L	N	S	B	E	G	T	M	I	S	T
M	E	H	Z	A	Y	I	P	T	P	O
J	S	E	Q	M	A	A	I	C	E	M
S	D	E	W	S	L	O	R	H	C	D
S	P	I	R	I	T	N	E	D	T	E
C	F	O	W	R	A	I	T	H	R	M
T	G	H	O	S	T	S	R	N	E	O
K	Y	B	S	K	E	L	E	T	O	N

Here's a tip: Some of the
words are written diagonally

25

Uninvited Ghosts

When the Browns moved to their new house they left the old one empty. The rooms were swept and bare. The windows had no curtains. The walls had pale squares where the pictures had been.

The new house was like that, too. It seemed quite empty. The Browns spent a dreadful day moving in. It was all fuss and bustle. Mrs Brown broke her best teapot. Mr Brown fell off a ladder. Simon (who was eight) put his foot through the bathroom floor. Marian (who was nine) lost her pencil set. The cat took one look and ran away.

A chest of drawers and two removal men got stuck on the stairs for half an hour.

At last, it was all done, and everybody was in a bad temper with everybody else. There was nothing but bread and margarine for supper. The cat came back and was sick on the kitchen floor. The television wouldn't work and the children were sent to bed.

It was then that they found the house was not empty.

First, Marian put her jersey in a drawer. She banged the drawer shut and a voice said "Ouch!"

Marian said to Simon, "I never touched you, stupid."

Simon said, "Stupid yourself!"

They were just about to get down to a proper battle, since both of them were tired and cross, when something else happened.

The drawer slid slowly open, and out came a pale grey shape, about three feet high, smelling of woodsmoke. It sat down on a chair and began to hum to itself. It looked like a bundle of bedclothes, except that it was not solid. You could see, quite clearly, the cushion on the chair underneath it.

Marian took one huge jump into bed and shrieked, "That's a ghost!"

The ghost said, "It's not nice to call people names. Be quiet and go to sleep."

It climbed on to the end of Simon's bed, took out a ball of wool and some needles and began to knit.

26

Have you ever tried telling your mother that you can't get to sleep because there is a ghost sitting on the end of your bed, clacking its knitting-needles? I shouldn't. She would probably say the sort of things that Mrs Brown said to Simon.

The trouble was, the ghost only appeared to Simon and Marian. "I like children," it said cosily, "always have. Eat up your dinner, there's a good boy." At this point it was sitting on the kitchen table, breathing down Simon's neck.

They couldn't get away from it. When they were watching television it sat itself down between them and talked loudly through all the best bits. When they wouldn't answer it poked them in the ribs. That was like being nudged by a damp, cold cloud. It trailed round the garden after them when they were playing. It made remarks when they were trying to do their homework. "Now then," it would say sternly, "no looking out of the window. No chewing the end of your pencil. When *I* was your age . . ."

"Go *away*, can't you!" yelled Simon. "This is our house now."

"No, it isn't," said the ghost smugly. "Always been here, I have. A hundred years or more. Seen plenty of families come and go, I have."

At the end of the first week the children woke up to find the ghost sitting on the wardrobe reading a newspaper. The newspaper had the date 1871 on it. The ghost was smoking a long white clay pipe. Beside it there was a second grey, cloudy shape.

"Morning," said the ghost. "Say how do you do to my Auntie Edna."

"She can't come here," roared the children.

"Oh yes, she can," said the ghost. "She always comes here in August. Likes a bit of a change, does Auntie."

Auntie Edna was even worse, if possible. She sucked peppermint drops which smelled so strong that Mrs Brown kept asking the children what they were eating. She sang hymns in a high, squeaky voice. She followed the children all over the house. She said she loved kiddies, it was nice to be where there were two such nice kiddies.

28

Two days later the children came up to bed to find a third ghost in their room. "Meet Uncle Charlie," said the first ghost. The children groaned.

"And Jip," said the ghost. "Here, Jip, good dog, say hallo, then."

A large grey dog that you could see straight through came out from under the bed, wagging its tail. The cat gave a howl and ran away again. The children howled too, with rage, and got under the bedclothes.

The ghosts chatted to each other all night, and told long boring stories.

The children decided that something had to be done. They couldn't go on like this. "We must get them to go and live somewhere else," said Marian.

The problem was where. And how.

That Sunday they were going to see their uncle, who lived by himself in a big house. Plenty of room for ghosts. The children were very cunning. They asked the ghosts if they would like a drive in the country.

The ghosts said it might make a bit of a change.

On the way, the three ghosts and their dog sat on the back shelf of the car. Mr and Mrs Brown kept asking why there was such a strong smell of peppermint drops. They asked why the children were so restless, too. The fact was the ghosts kept shoving them.

The ghosts liked it at Uncle Dick's. They liked his colour television and they liked his fitted carpets. Nice and comfy, they said. "Why not settle down here?" said Simon, in an offhand sort of way.

"Couldn't do that," said the ghosts. "No children. Dull. We like a place with a bit of life to it."

All the way home in the car they ate toast. There were real toast-crumbs on the car floor and the children got the blame.

Then the children had a brilliant idea. At the end of their road there lived a Mr and Mrs Clark, who had a baby. No other children. Just one baby. And all day long the baby was bored. It sat in its pram in the garden and threw its toys out and cried.

"I wonder . . ." said Simon and Marian to each other.

They made friends with Mrs Clark. They did her shopping for her and took the baby for walks and washed her car.

Mrs Clark invited them to tea.

They said to the ghosts, "Would you like to go visiting again?" The ghosts said they wouldn't mind.

Mrs Clark gave the children ham sandwiches and chocolate cake. The ghosts watched the colour television. They said it was a nice big one, and they liked the big squashy sofa too. They went all round the house and said it wasn't at all a bad little place. Nice and warm, they said. Homely.

They *loved* the baby. "Ah!" said Auntie Edna. "There now . . . bless its little heart. Give us a smile, then, darling." They all sat round it and chattered at it and sang to it and told it stories.

And the baby loved the ghosts. It cooed and chuckled and smiled and it never cried all afternoon. Mrs Clark said she couldn't think what had come over it.

Well, I expect you can guess what happened. The ghosts moved down the road. Mrs Clark has the happiest baby in the world, Simon and Marian no longer have to share their bedroom with three other people, and the cat has come back.

Penelope Lively

Illustrated by Shona Nunan

Divali

Each year, at about the end of October, Indians all over the world — in India itself, the West Indies, East Africa, Britain and Singapore, for example — celebrate the Hindu festival of Divali in different ways. It is a holiday and sometimes lasts for five days. Stories are told of how good triumphs over evil. Good deeds are like lights shining in the darkness, which is why Divali is known as the 'festival of lights'.

Hindus believe that God has no shape or form, but it is difficult to worship a god you cannot imagine. Also, they want to say so many things about God that one image is not enough. Therefore they worship the One God through many images, each one telling us something about Him. For example, Brahma speaks of God as creator, Krishna speaks of His love and Saraswati speaks of His wisdom.

There are many stories that describe the many qualities and activities of God. One story tells us how Krishna rescues Lakshmi from a wicked demon and so, in gratitude, Lakshmi visits families to bring them peace and wealth.

Another well-known story tells us how Prince Rama rescues his wife, Sita, from the ten-headed demon Ravana. Rama's stepmother banishes them both from the kingdom for fourteen years because she wants the throne for her son. When Sita is kidnapped by the demon, Rama and his friends rescue her. After fourteen years, they return to the kingdom. The people guide their way with divas. Divas are small clay bowls that are filled with oil. The small cotton wick inside the bowl is lit and the divas glow.

Divali IN INDIA

Rakesh and Shabhana help to paint the house and sweep the floors. While mother makes new clothes for the festival, father takes them shopping to buy boxes of sweets as presents for the family and friends. He also makes sure that he has paid all his bills. Once he has done this, Lakshmi will help him find prosperity in the coming year.

Shabhana paints geometric *rangoli* patterns in front of the door with coloured rice-flour paste and powdered chalks. Rakesh helps grandmother make wicks for the divas, which will be placed in every corner and on every ledge inside and outside the house. Now, Lakshmi will be pleased to visit them. Mother decorates a shrine to Lakshmi with flowers, fruit and coloured lights. The family thank God for all the gifts during the past year and pray for happiness, health and wealth in the coming year.

ressed in their new clothes, Rakesh and
habhana join in the street processions on
heir way to a mela (fair). They have been
ven some money to spend. What should
hey buy? Rakesh chooses some delicious
weets, and Shabhana chooses some lovely
lass bangles. They watch the snake charmers
nd then spend the rest of their money on an
lephant ride.

They watch a puppet show that tells the story
of Rama and Sita. Some of the children are
given masks, which represent the different
characters in the story. A storyteller recites
the story and the children mime it.

On their way to the firework display
they remember how father's Sikh
friend told them of Divali celebrations
in the Sikh Golden Temple at
Amritsar. Sikhs celebrate how one of
their great gurus (teachers) was set
free from prison at Divali. So
hundreds of fairy lights twinkle over
the pool surrounding the temple, and
huge catherine wheels are lit.

Rakesh and Shabhana rush to watch the
firework display. At the end, huge
puppets of the demon Ravana and his
wicked family, stuffed with fireworks, are
set alight.

Divali IN BRITAIN

In Britain, Divali is not a holiday and nights are cold, so it is often celebrated indoors on the Saturday or Sunday nearest to Divali. Houses are decorated with fairy lights. Prem and Kamali hang Divali cards on ribbons around the room before decorating the shrine.

It is time to visit the temple. The room inside is ablaze with fairy lights and decorations made from tinsel and coloured paper. Prem goes to watch the musicians, whilst Kamali joins in the singing, clapping her hands to the music. Everyone exchanges small presents of sweets and shares a meal in the temple kitchen.

Soon Prem and Kamali rush out into the courtyard. There is a bonfire and fireworks are lit. Many of their friends from school have come to join in the fun.

HAPPY DIVALI FESTIVAL OF LIGHTS

One year, as a special treat, Prem and Kamali were taken to a large park in Finchley, north London, where there was a mela. Suddenly, actors appeared with huge puppets of Rama, Sita and their friends, as well as the wicked Ravana. They performed the story, finishing with a very exciting battle. At the end, many of the children joined in!

A GHASTLY GHOSTLY PLAY

Characters

IT'S FULL OF ROTTEN RIDDLES

NARRATOR (a very small part, so a small person will do!)

THE GHOST FAMILY:

GRANDPA GERTIE
GRANDMA GWENDA
GLORIA MOTHER
GEORGIE FATHER
GREG GUS

WINNIE WITCH
SPOOKY SKELETON
ALEX, an ordinary boy (if you have one in the class!)
SETTING: A churchyard

Ideas for costumes:
Ghosts should wear large squares of white material with a hole cut in the centre for their heads. (Pieces of old white sheets are perfect.) Wear long white socks or tights so your feet and legs are white too and white woolly caps or scarves over your hair. The witch should have a black dress and black pointed hat. For the skeleton's costumes, stick white "bones" to a black jumper or top and tights. Alex wears a T-shirt and jeans under his piece of sheeting. He could also wear a cardboard ghost-mask.

NARRATOR: *(coming out in front of curtain)* Boo! Did I scare you?
AUDIENCE: No! *(Audience response doesn't affect Narrator's lines.)*
NARRATOR: Are you scared of ghosts, then?

38

AUDIENCE: No!

NARRATOR: Well, I'm going to take you to the churchyard where the Ghost family are having a picnic. (*curtain up*)

(*The ghost family is getting ready for a picnic.*)

MOTHER: Come on everyone. Help me set the things out.

(*She has a large picnic basket.*)

GRANDPA: Stop! It's no use. I've just counted and there are only ten of us. I refuse to sit down unless there are thirteen. Otherwise it's bad luck.

MOTHER: But Grandpa, I've worked all night getting your birthday picnic ready.

GLORIA: We've got all your favourites, Grandpa.

GUS: There's spook-etti, terri-fried eggs and ghoul-ash.

GERTIE: And for dessert we've got I-scream and boo-berry pie.

GRANDPA: I won't stay when there's only ten of us. You'll have to call the picnic off!

GRANDMA: He's right, you know. A friend of ours had a party with only twelve spooks and next night the house she was haunting burned down.

GEORGIE: Oo-oo-roast ghost!

GRANDPA: Don't be silly, George. She just flew up the chimney. But now she's out of work.

39

GRANDMA: After 429 years in the same job. Such a pity.

FATHER: Oh, very well. We won't start the party with only ten of us.

MOTHER: But what will we do?

FATHER: Find some more guests. Gwenda, Greg, Gus — float off and find someone to come to the party.

GWENDA: Okay, Dad. I'll see if Winnie Witch is home.

GREG: Good idea. And I'll waft over to Spooky Skeleton's to see if he's doing anything.

GUS: Who will I call on?

FATHER: Oh, just float around. You're sure to see someone you know. After all, it *is* Halloween.

(*Gwenda, Greg and Gus go off.*)

MOTHER: But that's why we haven't got thirteen at the party! Uncle Gavin and Auntie Genevieve and little Gordon are all out haunting tonight.

GLORIA: They'll find someone, Mum. Don't worry. Here, Grandpa, we've got a present for you.

(*She hands it to him.*)

GRANDPA: Just a minute. Let me find my spook-tacles. (*He unwraps the parcel.*) Well, thank you very much.

GRANDMA: What is it?

GRANDPA: It's called "Famous Haunters".

GERTIE: And it's by A. Spook.

40

GRANDPA: I do like a book about people I know.

(*Enter Gwenda and Winnie Witch. While they're all talking Grandma nods off.*)

GWENDA: Here's Winnie, so that's one more.

WINNIE: I was just wondering what I could do. My broomstick wouldn't start and there I was stuck at home — on Halloween too!

FATHER: Does it need a new handle?

WINNIE: I hope not. They're getting so expensive. I'm hoping the bristles just need cleaning. I'll take it to the garage tomorrow.

FATHER: I'd lend you our car, only it has to go to the garage too. The sheet belts are not working properly and it needs new spook plugs.

WINNIE: I do hope there's nothing much wrong with my broom. After all I've only had it 293 years.

GLORIA: Why don't you use your vacuum cleaner, Winnie?

WINNIE: The cord isn't long enough, Gloria. Besides, I'm old-fashioned. I only feel comfortable on a broom.

MOTHER: Never mind, Winnie. If it doesn't go, you can still use it to sweep the skeletons out of your cupboard.

WINNIE: Pesky things! They're always sneaking in there when I'm not looking.

(*Enter Greg and Spooky Skeleton.*)

41

GREG: Here we are, Spooky. Grandpa, Spooky was delighted to be asked to your party.

SPOOKY: Oh yes! I was sitting there feeling really miserable because I couldn't go to the Ball.

GERTIE: (*to Gloria*) It sounds like that story. "The Ghost of Cinderella".

MOTHER: Oh poor Spooky. Why couldn't you go to the Ball?

SPOOKY: I had no body to go with.

FATHER: Here, Spooky. Park your bones on this gravestone beside Winnie.

WINNIE: (*to Mother Ghost*) Yes, and I'll keep an eye on him in case he tries to sneak into any church cupboards.

(*Enter Gus and Alex.*)

GUS: Come on, don't be shy. Hey, Mum! Dad! I found this ghost sitting on a fence, so I asked him if he wanted to come to our picnic.

ALEX: I'm a bit confused. I was supposed to go to our class Halloween party in the church hall, but I got lost somehow in the mist. It's scary out there.

MOTHER: Well, never mind. You're quite safe here. Halloween is always a bit scary.

GRANDPA: (*grumpily*) It's all those humans running around.

ALEX: (*laughing politely*) Oh yes, Sir. Very funny!

GRANDPA: At least he's a polite, young ghost. Don't get many of those nowadays.

GEORGIE: (*to Gertie*) Don't let Grandpa get started on the Bad Old Days.

MOTHER: That will do, Georgie!

GERTIE: Oh, but Mum . . .

MOTHER: And you spook when you're spooken to, young lady.

GUS: (*to Alex*) That was Grandpa you spoke to. It's his birthday picnic. And this is Grandma, but she's asleep right now. And here are my mother and my father.

(*Mother and Father Ghost smile at Alex.*)

ALEX: Your parents and grandparents are great joining in like this.

GERTIE: (*puzzled*) Oh, we never have a picnic without them.

GUS: That's Gertie, my sister.

GERTIE: Would you like some boo-ble gum?

ALEX: No thanks. Not just now.

GUS: And these are my other sisters and brothers — Gloria and Gwenda and Georgie and Greg.

GREG: Hey, have you ever met Dracula?

ALEX: No, No, I haven't.

GREG: Just as well. He's a pain in the neck.

GWENDA: But his films are fang-tastic!

GEORGIE: There's someone new in our class at night school. He's got feathers and wings and fangs.

GLORIA: What's his name?

GEORGIE: Count Duck-ula!

ALEX: (*laughing*) That's really funny.

GEORGIE: (*surprised*) Is it?

GWENDA: (*pointing to Winnie*) This is our friend, Winnie.

WINNIE: (*to Alex*) How do you do? Badly, I hope. Would you mind holding my hat for a minute? (*She hands it to Alex.*) I want to put some scare-spray on my hair. (*She does this.*)

GREG: And this is another friend, Spooky.

SPOOKY: Isn't this fun? I'm going to have a rattling good time.

FATHER: And what's your name, my young friend?

ALEX: It's Alex, Sir.

GLORIA: That's a funny name for a ghost?

ALEX: (*thinking he gets it*) Oh, of course. We're supposed to have strange ones for Halloween, aren't we? Er . . . it's Grind-your-bones.

GLORIA: That's even weirder!

GRANDPA: (*impatiently*) Well, come along. Are you sure we're thirteen now?

FATHER: Yes, Grandpa, I've just counted.

GRANDMA: Then let's get started.

GUS: (*to Alex*) We always do the same things. First we have a General Knowledge Quiz.

GWENDA: Then we play Grandpa's favourite tape.

ALEX: What's that?

GWENDA: "Haunting Melodies!" Very dull!

GREG: But later on when he goes to sleep we put on "Tombstone Rock".

GERTIE: And play "Haunt and Seek" around the cemetery.

GLORIA: Sometimes we even manage to sneak off to the amusement park for a ride on the roller ghoster.

GEORGIE: Or the ghost train.

GRANDPA: Stop chattering, you children and let's start the quiz. I'm first.

GWENDA: (*whispering*) He always is.

GRANDPA: How do ghosts get through locked doors? Wake up, Grandma (*shaking her*). You know the answer to that.

GRANDMA: (*impatiently*) Of course I do, I wasn't really asleep. Just ghost-napping. The answer is, they use skeleton keys.

SPOOKY: So that's why my keys are always disappearing!

MOTHER: My turn. Why do black cats run across the cemetery?

ALL: (*together*) To get to the other side!

GREG: Oh, Mum, you always ask that one.

GLORIA: Me next. Who on the ghost ship said "Shiver my timbers"?

GUS: The skeleton crew!

SPOOKY: Nice chaps they are too.

GERTIE: What does a Red Indian ghost live in?

GEORGIE: A creepy teepee!

WINNIE: What kind of a horse does the headless horseman ride?

FATHER: Ah, that's an easy one, Winnie. A nightmare!

GREG: Hey, I've got one! What does a ghost use for a sore throat?

GWENDA: Coffin drops, of course.

GRANDMA: How much does a truck full of bones weigh?

WINNIE: (*quickly*) A skelly-tonne.

SPOOKY: (*sulkily*) You should have let me answer that.

GUS: Okay, Spooky here's one for you. What's a vampire's favourite soup?

SPOOKY: Scream of tomato.

FATHER: Well, that's about enough. Very good, children. Your general knowledge is improving a lot.

ALEX: (*laughing*) But those are just all riddles!

(*Everyone looks at him.*)

GRANDPA: There's something strange about him.

SPOOKY: You're right! I can feel it in my bones.

WINNIE: My thumbs are pricking all of a sudden.

GEORGIE: Mum, I'm scared!

MOTHER: Why the poor child's white as a sheet.

ALEX: Hey, you guys! It's just a joke, isn't it? Let's take off our disguises and have tea!

(*Alex pulls off his sheet and mask.*)

FATHER: A human! Disappear everyone! Quick, before it hurts us! (*They rush off stage.*)

46

(*Alex is left all alone.*)

ALEX: Wow! I can't believe it. They really were ghosts. That was a real witch. It can't be true. (*Speaks to audience*) Can it?

AUDIENCE: No!

ALEX: Oh good. I'll just go home and climb into bed. That must be where I really am. It's all a dream. Because there are no such things as ghosts. Are there?

AUDIENCE: No!

(*Alex walks off down through the audience. The others tiptoe back on stage.*)

MOTHER: Quick, pack up all our things and let's go off to the haunted house. We should be safe there.

FATHER: You know I never really believed in people before this. (*To audience*) But they *are* real, aren't they?

AUDIENCE: Yes!

FATHER: And we're not? You don't believe in us?

AUDIENCE: No!

FATHER: Well, we'll soon see about that. All right, gang. Line up. Now here we go.

(*The group lines up and then they too march off down through the audience, singing to the tune of "The Farmer's in the Dell".*)

ALL: A-haunting we will go, a-haunting we will go, Groaning high and moaning low, A-haunting we will go!

(*They disappear, except for Georgie who stops.*)

GEORGIE: See you around midnight — after we've visited Alex!

(*He runs off.*)

CURTAIN

Pat Edwards

Illustrated by Azoo

MAMARAGAN

The Thunder Man

Whenever the wet season clouds roll in across the south of northern Australia, that's the time to watch out for Mamaragan. For the billows of white cloud that form on top of the rain clouds are really huge white boulders and everyone knows that the thunder man just can't resist playing with them.

"Crack" he bangs two of them together and off shoot the sparks of lightning.

"Boom! Boom! Boom!" The rumble of his laughter shakes the sky and earth and all things on it.

But be grateful for his games, for this makes the clouds drop their rain on the thirsty land below and the rain, as you know, brings life and food to people and animals alike.

That's one of many Aboriginal myths once used to explain what caused thunder and lightning. Every culture in the world has similar stories. Some scary, some beautiful like the Arnhem Land one which says that thunder clouds are the home of tiny spirit children called the yurtus. When it rains the yurtus travel down to earth on the raindrops to search for human mothers.

None of the old myths is true, but they are often more interesting than the usual old ghost stories told during thunderstorms.

An Aboriginal story, retold and illustrated by Pat Edwards.

Just Imagine

Jane had too much imagination for her own good.
And the day came when it got her into real trouble . . .

It started at breakfast. Jane's father was so busy reading his paper that he was not paying attention to his scrambled eggs. Jane watched them slithering down his shirtfront and on to the table.

"He eats just like a pig!" she thought with disgust.

That was the first time it happened. Suddenly, in place of her father, Jane saw a pig sitting at the table! She was so startled that she jumped up, knocking her own plate to the floor.

"For goodness sake, Jane! Why don't you look what you're doing?" snapped her mother. "You spend far too much time daydreaming. Anybody who didn't know you would think you had the manners of a pig!"

"But it wasn't . . ." started Jane, pointing across the table. She stopped as she met her father's eyes peering over the top of his newspaper. "You wouldn't understand," she sighed.

"Probably not," said her mother. "Now go and change that skirt before you're late for school. You've spilt egg all over it."

At school, it happened again. Jane was sitting quietly in room eight gazing out of the window. It was a maths lesson with Miss Prigg, so, of course, she wasn't paying attention.

"You, child, stop daydreaming!" said Miss Prigg, who could never remember anyone's name.

Oh, it's you again! What's your name?"

"Jane Adams, Miss Prigg," said Jane politely.

"Well, Jane Adams, I've warned you before about daydreaming. One of these days it's going to get you into serious trouble."

"Old witch!" thought Jane. Then she jumped to her feet in horror. Miss Prigg was sailing round the room on a broomstick, chanting the seven times table. The class was in uproar. All the children were out of their seats, trying to dodge Miss Prigg as she zoomed over their heads. A moment later everything had returned to normal — well, almost. Miss Prigg and the children were back in their places, and Jane was on the floor with the contents of her desk scattered around her.

"Jane Adams! What have you been doing?" screeched Miss Prigg. "Pick those things up immediately. Now, children, we'll continue with the seven times table."

The room hushed and Jane, who was relieved to have got away with it so lightly, slid behind her desk and hoped that nobody would say anything to her for the rest of the lesson. As soon as the bell rang, she rushed into the playground, away from Miss Prigg's inquisitive gaze. She wanted to be by herself to think, but she was out of luck. She ran smack-bang into Billy Briggs, the school bully.

He really was a revolting boy! Jane couldn't remember ever seeing him without a runny nose and he never used a handkerchief to wipe it.

"What have you been up to, Adams?" asked Billy, leering forward and pinching Jane hard on the arm.

"None of your business, Briggs!" said Jane bravely. Then she thought, "I wonder?" and said aloud, "You watch yourself, Briggs, or I'll turn you into a . . ."

Even before she had finished saying it, Billy Briggs was the fattest, hairiest spider she had ever seen. Jane grinned with delight as she saw him trying to scuttle away.

"Should I step on him? No!" she decided. She had a much better idea.

She picked up the wriggling Billy by one of his legs, walked into the girls' toilets, and, giggling a little, held him over the sink. She turned the tap on full and watched the struggling spider going round and round as the water gurgled down the plughole.

"That's got rid of him," thought Jane with satisfaction. "Serves him right anyway."

At registration Jane looked all round the classroom, but Billy wasn't there. She began to feel uneasy. Surely she had gone too far this time. But just then there was a deafening wail and Billy Briggs burst into the room, dripping wet and sobbing. The class roared with laughter. Billy really was a sight!

"It was her. It was Jane Adams that did it!" Billy bawled.

"Don't be silly, Billy!" snapped Miss Prigg. "Jane's been here for the last ten minutes. You'll have to think of a better excuse than that for being late. I think you'd better explain yourself to the headmaster."

And she ushered him out of the room at arm's length.

Ten minutes later a grim-faced Miss Prigg arrived back in the classroom. "Come along, Jane, the headmaster wants to see you immediately," she said sharply. There was no chance to escape. Miss Prigg escorted Jane all the way to the headmaster's office, and even knocked on the heavy wooden door. What could she do? It was too late now.

The headmaster was looking at her in a most curious manner, while Billy Briggs stood in the corner sobbing. He was making a terrible mess of the head's new carpet.

"Now, Jane what's all this about?" said the headmaster. He sounded quite annoyed. Jane looked around desperately. What could she possibly say?

"Oh heck," thought Jane. "How am I going to get out of this one? I wish I wasn't here."

Then all of a sudden . . .

SHE WASN'T

Eunice McMullen
Illustrated by Nigel McMullen

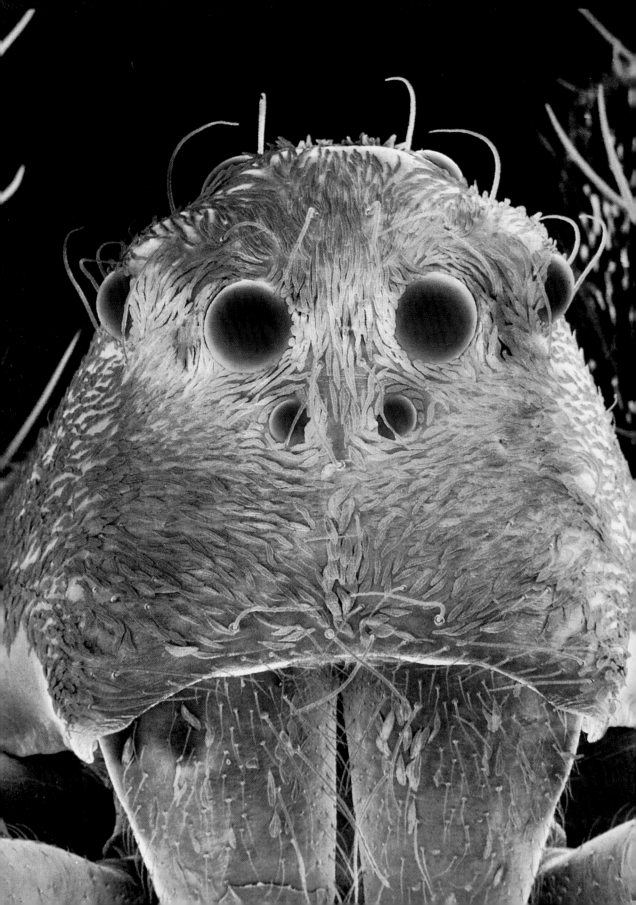

The Monster in the Garden!

Did I scare you?

Relax! You've nothing to worry about *unless* you're an insect. I'm just your common-or-garden old spider, very much magnified, of course.

Most people have a bad opinion of me. Some even shriek if I come near them and everyone seems to hate me building my web inside a house or shed. Yet, only a few of us can actually hurt humans. Most of us are busy, harmless little animals.

That's right — animals. We belong to the family called arachnids. (And if you're wondering where the name came from, just turn to page 58.)

Fairytales and folktales have helped to give me my bad reputation. Witches are usually shown in houses full of spiders' webs and we're often included as one of the ingredients in poisonous potions or spells. But there are just as many good stories, you know. An old superstition says that a spider on your clothes is a sign of good luck or of money to come. Another superstition is that you'll always thrive "if you let the spider run alive". Superstitions are usually based on a tiny grain of truth. We don't guarantee you money, but we help you because we kill many insects that would make your life a misery.
Think of that before you reach for a can of insect spray!

What are you weaving Arachne?

Who was Arachne?

A simple peasant girl, so the story goes — one who was a superb weaver of fine cloth. People from near and far came to marvel at the beauty and quality of her weaving and the praise went to Arachne's head. She began to boast that no one could match her.

Among the gods and goddesses living on Olympus was the goddess Minerva, who was the finest weaver of all. It did not take long for Arachne's reputation to reach her.

"A peasant girl claiming she is better than a goddess," she raged. "How dare she! I'll see she is humiliated and made to pay for her pride."

Minerva went to Arachne's humble cottage and challenged her to a contest. Great heaps of rainbow-coloured thread were piled in one corner, gold and silver thread in another and then the two set to work on their looms. Minerva produced a beautiful shimmering piece of cloth. But Arachne's cloth, which she finished at the same moment, was just as beautiful. No one could say which was better.

In a fit of temper, Minerva ripped Arachne's cloth from top to bottom, then beat the frightened girl about the head with her shuttle. Humiliated and shamed, Arachne hanged herself. For the first time Minerva felt pity. She sprinkled the girl's body with a magic liquid and changed her into a spider, so that Arachne could go on using her skill as a weaver.

Why do we remember such stories?

For a very good reason. Over the years, writers have borrowed the names of characters from the old Greek and Roman myths when they needed to invent new words or phrases. Scientists have done the same. When they were searching for a scientific name for spiders, scorpions and mites, they turned to the story of Arachne, the clever weaver, and called them all arachnids.

Wear a spider round your neck

There are many more good stories and sayings about spiders than bad ones. In fact, many people once believed that spiders had the power to cure illness.

Imagine how you would feel if your doctor told you that the cure for your fever was to wear a spider in a nutshell around your neck; or that you should swallow a mixture of frogs' eggs and spiders' webs to bring your temperature down! Yet, that's what people did!

One cure for an illness called jaundice was to swallow a live house spider rolled up in butter. Cruel, perhaps? Yes, especially for the poor harmless spider!

Do you remember the nursery rhyme about Miss Muffet? Miss Muffet's father was a doctor who experimented with spiders, as he was trying to find cures for colds and fevers. People were certain that spiders kept you healthy and so they carried them around in tiny boxes or nutshells for good health.

A spidery tale

According to an old story, a spider helped to keep a ruler of Prussia in good health. Frederick the Great ruled Prussia from 1712–86. Prussia was a state, roughly where northern Germany is today.

One day Frederick called for a cup of hot chocolate. Before drinking it, he put the cup on a table and went off to fetch a handkerchief. When he came back, he found a large spider had fallen from the ceiling into the chocolate.

"Bring me more chocolate," Frederick cried. A few moments later there was the sound of a gunshot from the kitchen. The cook had been bribed to poison his master. When the cook was asked to supply a second cup, he thought that the plot had been discovered, so he shot himself rather than risk being tortured. Ever since, the ceiling of the room in the palace apparently had a painting of a spider on it.

Pills and potions

Who invented medicine?

That's a question we can't answer. For as long as people have been on Earth, some people have been getting sick and other people have been trying to cure them. By studying bones that have been dug up at archeological sites, scientists have been able to prove that certain diseases have been around for a long time. Ancient records have also shown that early doctors knew a great deal about curing illnesses like colds and flu by using herbs — and a good dash of common sense.

In China, the Emperor Shen Nung who lived around 2700 BC put together a list of over one hundred herbal remedies. It is also believed that he or his surgeons invented the technique of acupuncture. In acupunture, tips of needles are inserted into the skin to stimulate the nerves. The oldest and greatest medical book in China is the *Nei Jing*. Its origins go back to the time of Emperor Huang Di who lived sometime between 2698–2599 BC, but it was put together by a number of people sometime between 403–221 BC. This book is still used today.

The early Chinese people were experts in the use of drugs made from plants, animals and insects. Ground-up cicada (insect) shells were used to treat fever and convulsions in children. Other medicines were made from fossilised bones and minerals such as iron.

and magic plants

The Aboriginal people in Australia, have a history that goes back at least as far as the Chinese and although they didn't have books, they were just as clever in the way they treated their sick. They were particularly good at healing injuries such as broken bones, burns and snake-bites and knew a great deal about using heat to ease toothache, fever and swelling. They used plants and trees to cure other illnesses such as headaches, dysentery and stomach-aches.

But other people also were experimenting with early kinds of medicine. The ancient Egyptians made lists of over 900 formulations and prescriptions. Some of the drugs they used in 1500 BC, such as castor oil and olive oil, opium and saffron (which both come from flowers), are still used today. Old writings tell us that Assyrians (who lived where northern Iraq is today) used over 300 drugs from plants, trees, herbs, roots, seeds, juices and minerals. Assyrian doctors also told their patients to use heat to help cure bruises, sprains or swellings.

In Europe, it was a Greek doctor named Hippocrates who first taught that it was important to observe the patient carefully before prescribing drugs. He is called the Father of Medicine by doctors who are trained in the European style of medicine and they take what is called the Hippocratic oath when they finish their training. It is a solemn promise that they will put their patient's well-being before everything else.

Each generation has learned from the one before and as people travelled from one country to another, they also learned from other cultures. The Indians had skilled doctors and so did the Aztecs, who lived in Mexico. Many Eastern countries realised, long before the Europeans, that cleanliness was an important part of being healthy.

In the last 100 years some useful drugs have been discovered.

Aspirin: To ease pain; first used in 1893 by a German doctor.

Paracetamol: To ease pain; introduced by a German doctor in 1893.

Antihistamines: Often used to help people with sinus problems or allergies like hay fever and wasp stings; first used in France in 1937.

Sulphonamides: Drugs used to fight bacteria; first used in 1937.

Penicillin: The first antibiotic to treat infection; discovered by Sir Alexander Fleming in 1928 and developed by an Australian scientist, Sir Howard Florey, in 1940.

Nowadays, doctors and pharmacists know how to prevent you getting some of the dangerous diseases that used to kill so many children in earlier times. Modern drugs can cure some illnesses more quickly and more easily.

Aloe

Liquorice

Tea-tree
or
Melaleuca

Eucalyptus

Olive

Garlic

Poppy

Foxglove

Magic plants

There are long lists of herbs that can cure or help people suffering from illnesses. Here are just a few of the ones you might have heard of.

Tea-tree or Melaleuca: the oil is good for cleaning cuts or scrapes and for rubbing on sore muscles.

Aloe: used in medicine to stop people from biting their nails and in burn ointments.

Liquorice: eaten as a sweet and also used in laxatives.

Eucalyptus tree: the oil is used to help clear up blocked noses and sinuses.

Olive: the oil is used in many medicines.

Garlic: often used to cure colds and flu.

Life-saving trees and plants

The cinchona tree or bush: the dried bark of this plant is used to make quinine, which is a cure for malaria. Malaria is an illness that attacks thousands of people living in tropical climates every year.

The foxglove: a drug called digitalis is made from its dried leaves and seeds. The drug is used in treatments for people with heart trouble.

The opium poppy: both morphine and codeine are made from the unripe seed heads of this plant. They are both used to relieve pain.

Lazy Tok

Tok was born lazy. When she was a baby, everybody said what a good baby she was because she never cried, but really she was too lazy to cry. It was too much trouble. The older she grew the lazier she became, until she got so lazy that she was too tired to go and look for food for herself. One day she was sitting by the side of the river, too lazy to wonder where her next meal was coming from, when a Nipah Tree on the other side of the river spoke to her.

"Good evening, Tok," he said. "Would you like to know how to get your meals without having to work for them?"

Tok was too lazy to answer, but she nodded her head.

"Well, come over here and I'll tell you," said the Nipah Tree.

"Oh, I'm much too weary to come over there. Couldn't you come over here?" yawned Tok.

"Very well," said the Nipah Tree, and he bent over the river.

"Just tear off one of my branches," he said.

"Oh, what a nuisance," said Tok. "Couldn't you shake one down yourself?"

So the Nipah Tree shook himself and down dropped one of his branches at Tok's feet.

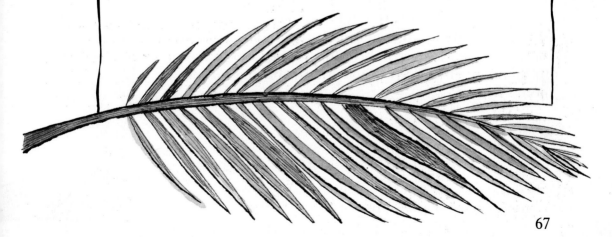

"Good evening, Tok," said the Nipah Branch. "Would you like to be able to get your meals without having to work for them?"

Tok was too lazy to answer, but she nodded her head.

"Well," said the Nipah Branch, "all you've got to do is to make a basket out of me."

"Good gracious," said Tok. "What a bother. Couldn't you make yourself into a basket without my help?"

"Oh, very well," said the Nipah Branch, and he made himself into a nice, neat, wide, fat basket.

"Good evening, Tok," said the Basket. "Would you like to be able to get your meals without having to work for them?"

Tok was too lazy to answer, but she nodded her head.

"Then pick me up and carry me to the edge of the road and leave me there."

"Good gracious me," said Tok, "do you think I'm a slave? Couldn't you pick yourself up and go without bothering me?"

"Oh, very well," said the Basket, and he picked himself up and went off and laid himself down by the side of the road.

He hadn't been waiting there long before a fat Chinaman came along.

"*Shen mao tung shi!**" said the Chinaman. "Here's a fine basket somebody has dropped. It will just do for me to carry my goods home from market in."

So he picked up the Basket and went off to market with it. He soon had it full of rice, potatoes, pumelos, durians, dried shrimps and other things too numerous to mention, and when it was full up he started off home with it.

* roughly translated means "What's that?"

After a while he felt hot and tired, so he put the Basket under a tree and went off to sleep. As soon as the Basket saw that the Chinaman was fast asleep, up it jumped and ran away back to Lazy Tok.

"Here I am," said the Basket. "Here I am, full to the brim. You have only to empty me out, and you will have enough food to last you a week."

"Dear, oh, dear!" said Lazy Tok. "What a bother. Couldn't you empty yourself out?"

"Oh, very well," said the Basket cheerfully, and he emptied himself into Lazy Tok's lap.

Next week, when Lazy Tok had eaten all the food, the Basket went off again and lay down on the grass by the side of the road. This time a Booloodoopy came along, and when he saw the Basket he thought it would be fine to carry his goods home from market; so he picked it up and took it off to the market. When it was full of pineapples and pumelos and all sorts of things too numerous to mention, he started off home with it, but he hadn't gone far before he felt tired and hot and sat down on the side of the road to have a nap. As soon as he had fallen asleep, up jumped the Basket and ran home to Lazy Tok.

So every week the Basket got itself carried to the market and came back full of fruit and rice and all sorts of other nice things too numerous to mention; and Lazy Tok sat on the river bank and ate and ate and ate and got fatter and fatter and lazier and lazier, until she became so fat and so lazy that she simply couldn't feed herself.

"Here we are waiting to be eaten," said the Fruit and the Shrimps and the other nice things one day.

"Oh, bother," said Lazy Tok. "Couldn't you feed me yourself, without giving me so much trouble?"

"We'll try," said the Fruit and the Shrimps and the other nice things; so after that they used to drop into her mouth without giving her any unnecessary trouble.

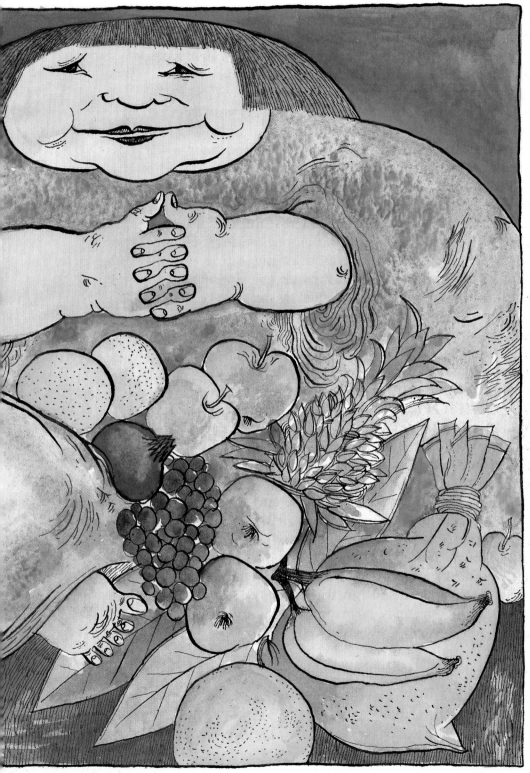

So Lazy Tok grew fatter and FATTER and FATTER and lazier and LAZIER and LAZIER, until one day the Basket went off to lie down by the side of the road, just when the fat Chinaman who had picked up the Basket the first time came along.

"Twee!" he said angrily. "There you are, you thieving scoundrel!" and he picked up the Basket and took it to the market to show all his friends what had been robbing them. All his friends came round and looked at the Basket and cried, "That is the rascal that has been robbing us!"

So they took the Basket and filled it full of soldier ants, lizards, hot-footed scorpions, bees, wasps, leeches and all sorts of other creeping, prickling, biting, stinging, tickling and itchy things far too unpleasant to mention; after which they let the Basket go.

Off ran the Basket with his load of bugs and beetles and centipedes and gnats and ran straight home to Lazy Tok.

"What have you got for me today?" asked Lazy Tok.

"You'd better get up and look," said the Basket.

"Oh, dear me, no!" said Tok. "I'm so tired, and I feel I couldn't stir a finger. Just empty yourself into my lap."

So ... the Basket emptied the ants and beetles and other things too horrible to mention into Lazy Tok's lap.

Lazy Tok got up and ran and ran and ran, as she had never run in her life before. But the ants, beetle and scorpions ran after her, and the leeches and lizards crawled after her, and the wasps and bees flew after her; and they stung her and bit her and pricked her; and the harder she ran the harder they bit her. As far as I know, she may be running still, and she is thinner than ever.

Mervyn Skipper

Illustrated by Jiri Tibok Novak

It's my home

Bristol

Bristolians recognise pictures of me in m tall stovepipe hat.

Isambard Kingdom Brunel

Clifton Suspension Bridge is famous all over the world and it was designed by Isambard Kingdom Brunel. After many problems building it, the bridge was finally opened on December 8th, 1864 — five years after Brunel's death. The most famous story about this bridge concerns a young woman in Victorian times. She decided to kill herself by jumping off the bridge. But the wide skirt of her crinoline dress acted like a parachute and she landed safely in the mud below!

Soon the Great Western Steamship Company was bor Brunel was asked to design a steamship to cross the Atlanti Ocean to America. He built three: the Great Western, the Great Britain and the Great Eastern. Thirty thousa people watched as the Great Britain was launched in Brist on July 9th, 1843. Today, you can visit this famous ship in Bristol Docks, where she is being restored.

Brunel was a brilliant engineer who designed the first railway line from Bristol to London which included the two-mile-long Box tunnel near Bath. He built other lines for the Great Western Railway Company.

In the old days, Bristol was a famous port — one of the biggest in the country. Sailing ships used to come right into the centre of the city to unload their cargoes.

Today, ships use the modern docks at Avonmouth and the city centre looks very different! The river where ships once docked now goes underneath it.

Ship-shape and Bristol fashion, as we used to say! Do you know what it means?

I can't see Wales, let alone America!

Cabot Tower on Brandon Hill

Some people think it was Columbus who discovered America, but any Bristolian will tell you it wasn't him — it was John Cabot. Cabot sailed from Bristol in his tiny sailing ship, the *Matthew* with its crew of fourteen. He reached America on June 24th, 1497.

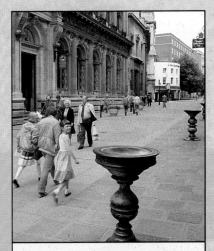

Pay on the nail is another famous Bristol expression which means to pay cash for something. In the old days, merchants used to buy and sell corn at the Corn Exchange. They agreed their price and then handed over the cash on the *nails* outside the building. The nails are still there today.

The Toothpaste Genie

Most genies come in magic lamps — but not Amanda's! Most genies grant wishes immediately — but not Amanda's!

Amanda found her genie in a toothpaste tube. He's an apprentice genie, which means he's not yet fully qualified. And he's a bit lazy. But Amanda desperately wants her own horse . . .

"I want a horse."

"A horse?"

"Yes, a horse. You know, a horse."

"I do? I know a horse?"

"What's with you? Everyone knows what a horse is. Four legs and a mane and tail. You ride them."

"I'm not *everyone*. I'm *me*." The genie rubbed his eyes and yawned again. Amanda wasn't sure if he really didn't know what a horse was or if he was pretending to be stupid because it was early. But he said, "Sounds like the sort of wish the Master Genie likes," so she felt relieved.

"I want Flame," she said.

"But you said you wanted a horse." The genie looked genuinely puzzled.

"I want a horse like Flame."

"Jumping Geniacs, Amanda, I can't do that."

"Why not?"

"You didn't say 'I wish.' "

"I *wish* you'd make me a horse like Flame. Please."

"Still can't."

"Oh, come on. Why not now?"

"I don't know what a 'Flame' horse looks like."

"Oh, is that all? Flame is a stallion the colour of his name. He's huge — really huge. And fierce. He won't let anyone ride him but me and with me he's as gentle as a lamb."

"Okay, there you go," the genie said.

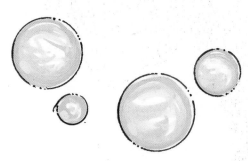

As Amanda watched, her anticipation changed to fear. In the far corner of her bedroom was an animal so tall its ears brushed the ceiling. It was covered with red and gold spots and with each breath fire sprang from its nostrils. It might have been a dragon for all Amanda knew. It certainly wasn't a horse.

When it caught sight of her crouching behind the closet door it gave a snort of recognition that singed the bedspread and started towards her. She wanted to close herself in the closet but she was so scared her hands slipped on the doorknob. The thing tripped over the desk leg, stomped on her doll house, then laid its head on Amanda's knee and immediately changed into a sort of giant lamb.

The thing's affectionate nuzzling pressed wads of smelly wool into her mouth and nostrils until Amanda thought she was going to suffocate. With difficulty she managed to turn her head sideways. In her hand was the toothpaste tube with an extremely small bubble at the top. She could see the genie staring at his creation.

"Make it go away!" Amanda screamed through the wool.

"I think it's very good." The genie's voice was as tiny as his bubble. "We're graded on size and originality."

"I don't care. It's going to kill me!"

"No, no, it's gentle as a lamb with you, remember?"

Amanda was desperate. The thing was pressing against her so firmly she'd lost the feeling in her legs. Now it began to rub its head up and down her chest, but it was so strong it only succeeded in rubbing her up and down the wall.

"If my mum comes in you'll get it," Amanda gasped. "She'll make you pose."

The genie's size increased a little and he peered at her anxiously. "Do you think she would?"

"I'm positive! And if she doesn't I'll take the cap off every hour and squeeze your tube so you'll never get any sleep!"

"Oh, all right, but it's the most sensational thing I've done."

Amanda collapsed with relief as the thing vanished. She was lying there catching her breath when she saw that the genie's bubble was disappearing. "Oh, no, you don't!" She squeezed the tube angrily. "I still don't have my horse!"

The genie popped back up. "What do you mean? I've granted your wish for the day. As a matter of fact, I've granted two. And I can't even put it in my report!" He looked as if he would cry.

"Why not?"

"We can't take credit for something that would harm our owners," he quoted. "And I guess that animal could have killed you with kindness."

"It's too bad you can't put it in your report. It *was* pretty fantastic." Amanda smiled. "But you could take credit for a real horse, couldn't you?"

"I suppose so," the genie replied sulkily, "but that's commonplace. And I did give you exactly what you described!"

"You know I meant one I could ride!"

"No, I didn't. Anyway, there's no point talking about it. That's your wish for today."

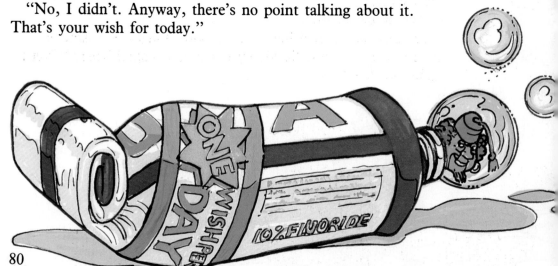

"*No!*" Amanda shouted to keep him from disappearing. "It's not my wish if you can't put it in your report."

The genie looked at her. "But it says just one on my label. I didn't write the label. That's the rules. And I'm getting sleepy. We need a lot of sleep, you know."

"I know, I know. You keep telling me. But you also need something to put in your report. Why don't we start all over again?"

The genie sucked on his pipe, which had gone out. He stared at it, then very slowly and deliberately flicked his finger and thumb together to produce a light. Amanda forgot and bit her fingernail. She watched as it grew.

"We — ll," — the genie dragged out the word as though it were the biggest *well* in the world — "I guess if I can't report it, it doesn't count."

"Whew," Amanda sighed.

"But I gave you exactly what you described. You'll have to be more accurate."

"Can't you read minds? I thought you said genies could."

The genie looked embarrassed. "Apprentices aren't supposed to. That's for when we graduate. But I do know how," he admitted.

Amanda smiled, and he smiled back. It was the first time he had smiled directly at her, the first time they had shared a smile. His was rather sly, but still, a smile was a smile.

"I'll make a picture of Flame in my mind and you can copy him, okay?"

The genie nodded.

Amanda scrunched her eyes up and thought of Flame as clearly as she could. Suddenly her eyes snapped open. "Don't make him here —"

81

But it was too late. The genie had disappeared.

Then Amanda forgot everything in the thrill of looking at her horse. He stood in the middle of the room, definitely chestnut, definitely a stallion, with a noble head and ears pricked forward, with deep, warm, dark brown, intelligent eyes watching her. He was wearing an English saddle and bridle.

"Oh, Flame."

He whinnied in reply. Amanda stood beside him, patting his neck while he nuzzled her pockets. He was exactly the right horse. "Thank you, you marvellous genie," she whispered.

"Amanda! Come for breakfast!"

Flame started. Amanda put her hand over his nose in case he decided to whinny again.

"Amanda!"

"Coming!" What am I going to do? she thought, stepping into the hall and closing the bedroom door tightly. Then she opened it again. Maybe while her parents were eating would be the best time to get Flame out of the house. But from the kitchen table they could see into the back yard. And she couldn't leave him in the front of the house; he might wander down the road or a neighbour might see him. She closed the door again. Maybe she would have a better chance of getting him out of the house after breakfast. Sometimes her parents went shopping on Saturdays. Why hadn't the genie made Flame appear outside?

"*Amanda!*"

"Coming!" Move him now or later? It was too late. Mrs. Atkins was at the end of the hall. Flame would have to stay in the bedroom until she could think of some way to get him out. "I was just coming." Amanda scooted into her place so fast she knocked over her glass of milk. "Sorry," she said, getting the dishcloth.

Her parents looked at each other, then started to laugh. "That's more like the old Amanda," her father chuckled. "You've been pretty strange all week. It's nice to see you can do something normal."

Amanda stood still, not sure whether that was a compliment or not. But at least her parents weren't angry with her.

Suddenly there was a terrific noise from the direction of her bedroom. "What was that?" her mother asked.

Amanda swung around and the cloth in her hand sent the jug of pancake syrup crashing to the floor.

"Now look what you've done!" her father said, grabbing the cloth.

"What was that noise?" Mrs. Atkins repeated.

"Um, must have been some books."

"Sounded like the whole library," her father said.

Amanda stuffed some pancake into her mouth. If only she could get back to Flame before he decided to whinny.

"Stop eating and clean up that mess," Mr. Atkins ordered. "Once is an accident, but twice is a mess!"

"Not that way!" This time her mother grabbed the cloth. "I'd better do it. You just eat."

"She should clean up her own messes," her father began.

Amanda had so much pancake in her mouth she couldn't chew. Maybe her parents would argue and she could get Flame outside.

"She'll just make more mess," Mrs. Atkins said.

"I suppose so." Mr. Atkins went into the living room, the newspaper under his arm.

"I'm finished, Mum," Amanda said. Even if her parents weren't going to have an argument, it would be her only chance to move Flame before he gave everything away. Her father's favourite chair faced away from the hall, and her mother was getting ready to wash the kitchen floor. But just then there was a whinny. Abruptly Amanda opened her mouth and bellowed, "Whewhewheee."

Mrs. Atkins jumped. "What was that for?"

"I'm a horse." Amanda cantered twice around the kitchen, then galloped through the living room and down the hall to her bedroom.

Flame had knocked over the chair to her desk. When Amanda opened the door he looked up and his leg became stuck in the chair rungs. He clattered backwards into the bookcase, snorting with fear and making the most awful noise.

"Whoa, boy," Amanda said soothingly, and as he quieted she lifted the chair away from his leg. Quickly she gathered the reins and stuck her head out the door to see if the way was clear.

Just then Mr. Atkins shouted from the living room, "You do sound convincing, Amanda. I'd almost swear you had a real horse in there!"

"I'm getting better at it!" she shouted back, then quietly to Flame, "Come on." She tugged his reins and started down the hall to the den, whinnying again to cover up the noise Flame's hoofs made even on the carpet. "Thank heaven my bedroom's not upstairs," she thought.

Suddenly Amanda pulled the horse into the bathroom, crashed the door shut and turned the lock. Not any too soon, for her mother was also heading for the bathroom.

"Really, Amanda," Mrs. Atkins said, "if you're going to be a horse, will you please go outside. Horses don't belong in houses. I can't think with all that clattering! What *do* you have on your feet?"

"Sorry!" Amanda yelled. Flame had managed to wedge himself sideways between the sink and the bathtub. She pushed his flank and pulled on the bridle. "I'm just getting ready to go out!" Amanda held her breath and put her hand over Flame's nostrils in case he decided to join in the conversation.

"Are you sure you're all right?" Mrs. Atkins tried the doorknob.

"I'm fine — oof!" Flame had butted her with his head.

Amanda waited a little longer. Finally she heard her mother going back to the kitchen. She waited another few minutes, then quietly slipped open the door. The den was just a few more paces down the hall. She started to lead Flame out, then she sniffed. The essence of horse was overpowering. The bathroom smelled distinctly like a stable. Amanda got out the can of air-freshener and sprayed. At least now it smelled like a stable in a pine forest.

Holding Flame firmly by the bridle she led him into the den and through the sliding glass door onto the patio. Then she pulled him around the side of the house before her mother could look out the window. Flame began to eat the grass. She tied him securely to the fence.

Frances Duncan

Illustrated by G.A.S.S.P.

How does the Tooth paste get in the Tube?

(And other fascinating facts!)

Amanda's genie went in and out of his toothpaste tube through the top.
And toothpaste comes out of the tube at the top.
But how does it get in?
   Simple! Through the bottom!

From toothpick to toothbrush

Caring for our teeth has always been important. We grow a set of adult teeth when we lose our "baby teeth", but after that we can't grow new ones to replace those we lose — unlike some animals. If you were living at the time when people were mainly hunters of wild animals, teeth lost might have led to starvation.

The toothpick was the first tool for cleaning teeth. People used short sharp bits of wood to dislodge those pieces of food that got stuck uncomfortably in their teeth. Gold toothpicks were sometimes used by wealthy people, from the time of Ancient Egypt right down to recent times.

Wooden pencils, with special fibre at the tip, were also developed but they couldn't reach the "hard-to-get" spots or clean between teeth.

The first toothbrushes were made 500 years ago and pigs' hair was used as bristle. Toothbrushes have changed a great deal since then. Today, when used with dental floss, they are effective tools to help you fight tooth decay.

From powder to paste
The first toothpaste was a powder, not a paste! It came in tins and jars. You had to wet the powder by dipping your wet toothbrush in the tin or jar; or you could put some powder on the brush and then wet it. It was messy!

In 1908 the collapsible tube was invented and tooth powder became toothpaste!

Toothpaste — what's it made of?
The first toothpastes were often made of sweet and sticky ingredients to make toothpaste taste nice! This did more to help tooth decay then prevent it! Today, there are seven major substances in toothpaste:

1 **fluoride** — toughens the enamel on your teeth against attack by the acids in your mouth.

2 **polish** — to clean as well as polish.

3 **foaming agent** — ever wondered why toothpaste turns to foam as you brush? That's because of the foaming agent. The foam loosens the tiny bits of food which cling to your teeth and it holds the bits until you rinse your mouth.

4 **humectants** — the word "humid" means "moist". Humectants keep toothpaste soft and moist. Otherwise it would harden in the tube.

5 **binding agents** — these "hold" all other ingredients together and stop them from separating into liquids and solids.

6   flavour — to give your mouth a fresh, clean taste.
Herbs such as peppermint or spearmint are used.

7   colour — to make toothpaste look attractive and to
identify different types. Blue, pink and white are the common
colours.

And the tube?

Toothpaste was packed in aluminium tubes but nowadays a type
of plastic tube is mostly used. These tubes keep their shape and are
less easily damaged.

Sometimes you will come across "pump packs". Put your brush
under the tap, press the pump and a blob of paste drops onto the
bristles.

And how does toothpaste get in the tube?

The upside-down tubes pass along a conveyor belt and are filled
by a special "filling head". Then, they are heat sealed, or "crimped"
shut, by special machines.

And what about the stripes?

Separate "filling heads" fill the different colours and the toothpaste is
carefully manufactured to ensure the colours don't mix when inside
the tube. If you could cut a tube in two, without squashing it, you
would see the colours inside.

What causes tooth decay?

Believe it or not, your mouth is home for thousands of bacteria. And
they just love to feed on the carbohydrates in lollies and sweet food.
The sweeter and stickier the food, the more the bacteria like it!

Plaque is an invisible, sticky, spongy film, full of bacteria,
which covers your teeth. You can see it if you chew a special tablet which
you can get from your dentist or your chemist. These tablets make the plaque
turn pink so you can see what you have to brush away.

When you eat food with carbohydrates, especially the sticky ones that cling
to your teeth, the bacteria use the carbohydrates and the saliva in your mouth
to create an acid. This acid attacks the enamel of the tooth, making a hole in it
. . . a hole which can get bigger and deeper. So it's your job to shift the plaque
as quickly and as often as you can.

The greatest damage is done in the first twenty minutes after you have
eaten. Brush your teeth after meals and especially before you go to bed.
Otherwise, acid will be attacking your teeth all night while you sleep!

Did you know?
No two sets of teeth are the same. A dental x-ray is as unique as a fingerprint. A hungry robber in an American grocery shop, munched a piece of cheese during a hold-up. Experts examined the cheese and described exactly the mouth that nibbled it. Faced with the evidence, the man confessed!

OH I WISH I'D LOOKED AFTER ME TEETH

Oh, I wish I'd looked after me teeth,
  And spotted the perils beneath,
All the toffees I chewed,
  And the sweet sticky food,
Oh, I wish I'd looked after me teeth.

I wish I'd been that much more willin'
  When I had more tooth there than fillin'
To pass up gobstoppers,
  From respect to me choppers
And to buy something else with me shillin'.

When I think of the lollies I licked.
  And the liquorice allsorts I picked
Sherbet dabs, big and little,
  All that hard peanut brittle,
My conscience gets horribly pricked.

My Mother, she told me no end,
  "If you got a tooth, you got a friend,"
I was young then, and careless,
  My toothbrush was hairless,
I never had much time to spend.

92

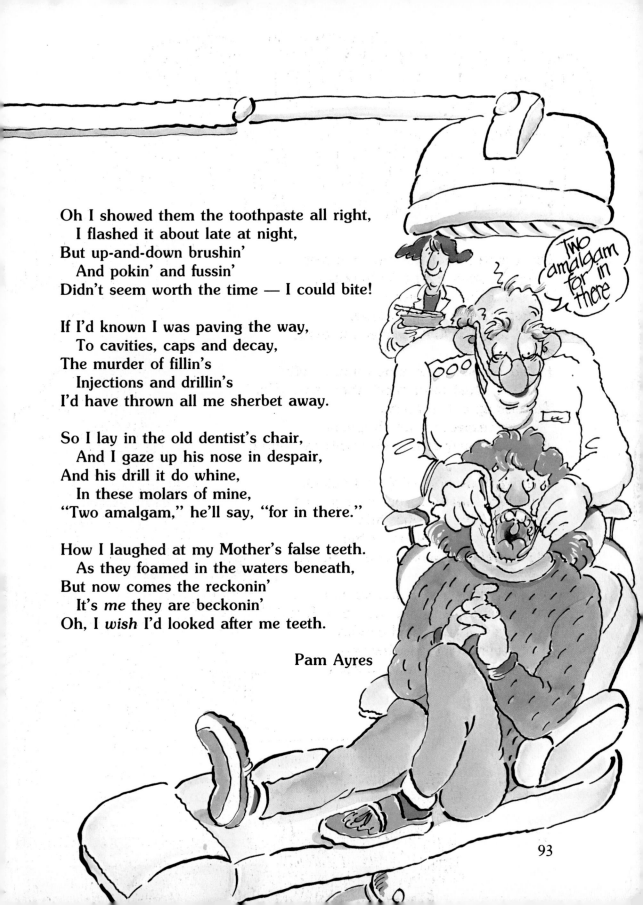

Oh I showed them the toothpaste all right,
  I flashed it about late at night,
But up-and-down brushin'
  And pokin' and fussin'
Didn't seem worth the time — I could bite!

If I'd known I was paving the way,
  To cavities, caps and decay,
The murder of fillin's
  Injections and drillin's
I'd have thrown all me sherbet away.

So I lay in the old dentist's chair,
  And I gaze up his nose in despair,
And his drill it do whine,
  In these molars of mine,
"Two amalgam," he'll say, "for in there."

How I laughed at my Mother's false teeth.
  As they foamed in the waters beneath,
But now comes the reckonin'
  It's *me* they are beckonin'
Oh, I *wish* I'd looked after me teeth.

                              Pam Ayres

IT'S YOUR DECISION!

How to lose your teeth

1 Never brush them.

2 Let plaque attack your teeth all night.

3 Only go to the dentist when you cannot put up with the toothache any longer.

4 Feed the bacteria in your mouth with lots of gooey, sticky sweets.

How not to lose your teeth

1 Brush, using the correct method, after every meal.

2 Use dental floss and a toothbrush every night before you go to bed.

3 Visit the dentist regularly. Let him be the detective who can spot early signs of tooth decay.

4 Eat food which builds strong teeth and healthy gums: fruits, vegetables, meat, fish, eggs, nuts, etc.

WORDS TO KEEP BEFORE YOU LOSE THEM

GLOSSARY

I KEPT MY TEETH

Glossary

aluminium (*p. 90*)
a light, silver metal

amalgam (*p. 93*)
fillings

anticipation (*p. 79*)
waiting for
something to
happen

apple-pie order (*p. 22*)
a saying that
means everything
is very tidy

I LOST MINE

archaeological sites (*p. 62*)
places where
people dig up the
remains of ancient
people and the
things they used in
their lives

Arnhem Land (*p. 48*)
a region in the
Northern
Territory of
Australia

castor oil (*p. 63*)
an oil used as a
medicine

cavities (*p. 93*)
holes

I WAS HALF-HEARTED ABOUT IT

convulsions (*p. 62*)
violent, sudden
movements of the
body

crinoline (*p. 74*)
an underskirt
made of stiff
material which
makes the dress
worn over the top
swell out

95

dislodge *(p. 88)*
move something from its position

durian *(p. 68)*
a large, oval tropical fruit with a prickly rind; tastes nice but smells awful

dysentery *(p. 63)*
a painful disease that makes you go to the toilet a lot

essence *(p. 87)*
scent; smell

formulations and prescriptions *(p. 63)*
medical treatments for people's illnesses

fossilised *(p. 62)*
things that have become fossils

haggard *(p. 21)*
old and tired

humiliated *(p. 58)*
shown up in front of other people

jaundice *(p. 60)*
a disease that turns skin and eyes a yellowish colour

marvel *(p. 58)*
to be amazed at

mineral *(p. 63)*
substance that is formed naturally in the earth (e.g. salt, coal)

mites *(p. 59)*
small, insect-like creatures

perils *(p. 92)*
dangers

pharmacist *(p. 65)*
a person who makes up medicines and drugs to help people get better

pumelo *(p. 68)*
a type of fruit with a refreshing taste that looks like a large green-skinned orange

quieted *(p. 85)*
an American expression meaning the horse becomes quiet

reproachfully *(p. 19)*
to blame someone in a sad not an angry way

singed *(p. 79)*
to burn slightly

sinus *(p. 65)*
air passage in the nose

stimulate *(p. 62)*
to excite; arouse

ushered *(p. 54)*
showed him the way

whinny *(p. 83)*
to make a gentle snort

WHAT HELPS KEEP YOUR TEETH TOGETHER?

TOOTHPASTE

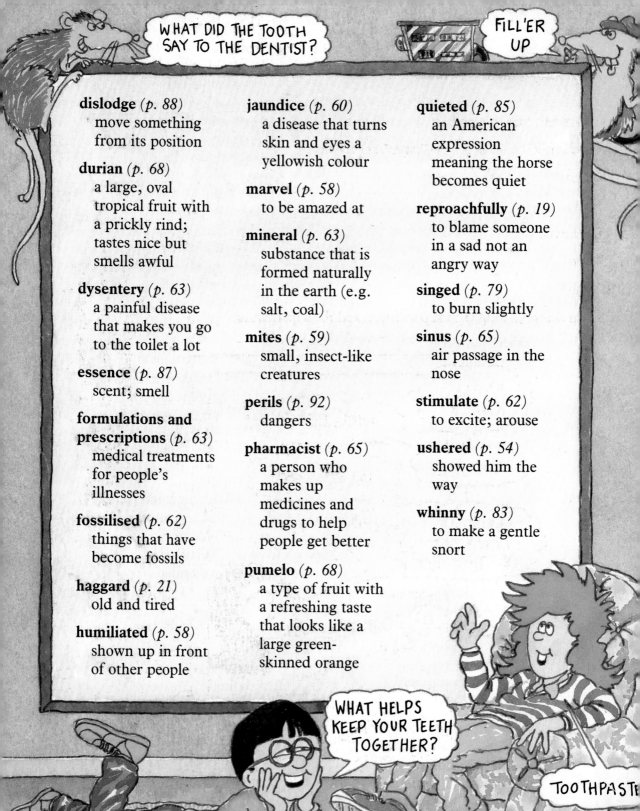